163 Days

To the NHS – Cleaners, Porters, Administrators, Health Care Assistants, Nurses and Doctors. I want to say more than a 'thank you' for saving my life repeatedly and offering the highest level of care with a smile. I wouldn't be here without you.

163 Days

Hannah Hodgson

Seren is the book imprint of
Poetry Wales Press Ltd.
Suite 6, 4 Derwen Road, Bridgend, Wales, CF31 1LH
www.serenbooks.com
facebook.com/SerenBooks
twitter@SerenBooks

The right of Hannah Hodgson to be identified as
the author of this work has been asserted in accordance
with the Copyright, Designs and Patents Act, 1988.

ISBN: 978-1-78172-647-1
ebook: 978-1-78172-649-5

A CIP record for this title is available from the British Library.

The poems in this book are creative works by Hannah Hodgson,
not a non-fiction account.

The publisher acknowledges the financial assistance of the Books Council of Wales.

Cover artwork: Over Coral – Credit: Artist Sue Austin
– Photo Norman Lomax – © We Are Freewheeling Ltd

Printed in Bembo by Severn, Gloucester.

Contents

163 Days

Monday 19th January

After four and a half hours I'm seen in A&E,
by a registrar who rolls her eyes when I cry
as she gives me my first cannular.
I feel as a tin must, when an opener
pries a portion of its lid.

16 y/o female with a history of gastroesophageal reflux attended A&E. Previously seen by Dr Sanai at Magdalena Hall age 9, & managed at a local level. Transferred from RLI today by car, she was ambulatory although fainted in waiting room. Parents were also in attendance. History includes accelerated weight loss and vomiting. Pregnancy test negative. Bowel sounds not present & obvious dehydration. Admitted to gastro, query neuro & surgical review in the morning.

Tuesday 20th January

A heart monitor the size of a portable TV,
oxygen valve with orange BB pellet,
blankets which smell of vinegar,
a whiteboard with my name on.

Bloods = deficiency of potassium, magnesium, sodium, iron & folic acid, rapid infusions ongoing. Vomit and urine outputs higher than intake. 2 blue cannulas (veins delicate, wide bore not appropriate), blood pressure very low; X-rays show small blockage in bowel. Picolax prescribed today. Patient describes past colonoscopy in which this therapeutic failed. I informed her of hospital treatment protocols. Review her again tomorrow.

Wednesday 21st January

For days, my mouth has bubbled
like a cauldron, unable to pronounce
words before they pop.

Patient pale & still has very low blood pressure. She's withdrawn, psychology referral to ensure this presentation is entirely physical. Veins collapsing frequent cannulation. CT ordered for exclusion of brain tumour, brain lacerations, abdominal tumour, significant bleed etc.

Thursday 22nd January

My body has become a singular organ
rejecting its surroundings, but unable
to survive without them.

Little improvement in bloods, and blood pressure continues to be low. Pulse is regular but tachycardic. Previous endoscopy revealed duodenal ulcers. Query escalation in care required.

Friday 23rd January

My anatomy is screaming incoherently,
desperate in this disaster zone.
Doctors struggle to decide
which area to triage first.

Kidney function borderline concerning, bloods to be drawn every 6 hours. Introduced additional intravenous fluids with glucose. White blood cells 0.7. Patient not on any therapeutics that would offer a cause of this. If it continues into tomorrow isolation will be essential. Bleep overnight reg. if she's showing signs of sepsis.

Sunday 25th January

The cannula tissues, my remaining veins
so tiny they use a yellow one from neonatal.
This bursts after an hour. A saline
water balloon slowly inflates
beneath my skin. The nurse's voice
insinuates I pulled it out.

Dr Naseeb from psychology assessed Hannah and seems to believe this isn't from an eating disorder. She notes that Hannah has no marks on her knuckles indicating bulimia, and her weight is slightly above average BMI, with no indications of phycological disorder. Dr N. is interested in her presentation and will follow up on patient before discharge.

Monday 26th January

My friends have sent cards — I put them on the wall
in a triangular bird formation.
Infection Control arrives on the ward, order them down.

PHE ENGLAND NOTICE OF REMOVAL OF PRODUCTS WHICH COULD INHIBIT THE ABILITY TO PREVENT INFECTION SPREAD

Wednesday 28th January

I hand over my two-litre tub with screw lid,
the kind primary schools use for bulk
purchase PVA glue. My collage
of life for 10 days enclosed, protocol
chopped apart, my needs falling
away like unsecured glitter.

NHS acronym of patient needs
P – Physical   /   I
I – Intellectual   /   want
E – Emotional   /   to go
S – Social   /   home.

Patient continues to vomit. It appears to be effortless and wakes her frequently throughout the night. Bloods are improving, electrolytes stable although iron values remain low. Crossmatch type is on file, but as there is scant evidence of a bleed, and little evidence a transfusion would be useful.

Friday 30th January

I eat a cheese and tuna toastie
for whom I'm home
for less than two hours.

Patient given canteen voucher to choose what she would like to eat. Both eating and aftermath was observed. Vomit weighed 472g, and she had no control over emesis.

Saturday 31st January

The 7-year-old in the next bed along was impaled
through his eye, just missing his brain. He smiles at me.
His lashes trapped under the tape
of his eyepatch like a taxidermy butterfly.

As of last night she has been nil by mouth, which has come along with blood glucose dips, prescribed sublingual paste which was spat out once result achieved. Referred for Naso-gastric tube as bloods are again deteriorating and will soon be indicative of Total Parenteral Nutrition which is a risky treatment option.

Sunday 1st February

Every day the nurses check the china cup of my body,
chart its chipping, its physical loss.

>7kg in past 7 days, mainly fat burnt but some muscle wastage. We've encouraged her to exercise, but her palpitations along with low blood pressure present difficulties.

Tuesday 3rd February

I'm a farmer with a plough,
as strands of hair bundle together
on my brush. I show my tumble weeds

to The Consultant, who says "it's to be expected"
and leaves without saying anything else.

> Moderate hair loss due to malnutrition, along with white ridges appearing on nails. Vomiting persists. It's becoming evident that nasogastric tube is ineffective. We should consider moving the tube down into her bowel to make Naso-Jejunal (NJ) our next treatment option.

Wednesday 4th February

It's winter inside my bones,
this body a snow globe.
My scars are purple,
my faith in medicine frozen.
I try to bring it to temperature slowly
before it shatters out of existence.

> Low Blood Pressure. Fainting. Vomiting. No change.

Friday 6th February

"You're too young and pretty to be this ill," The Consultant says.
As if an emergency warrants a compliment.
"You're a lot shorter than you should be though,
percentile-wise." I blink. Tell him
about the tongue swelling in my airway. I ask
if he could kindly add the offending drug to my list
of allergens and prescribe reversal medication.

> ~~Cyclizine TDS 25mg~~ Ondansetron QDS.

Saturday 7th February

In the next bed along, there's a three-year-old
whose bones poke out like cutlery on a table, covered by cloth.

> I explained to both the patient and her mother that recent blood results – chronic B12 Deficiency and Acute Iron deficiency, probable neutropenia.

Sunday 8th February

I'm in x-ray, a tube with a metal guidewire
pushed up my nose, down my throat
through my stomach and into my bowel.
A mail chute deployed on prescription
delivering parcels of nutrition.

> Successful Naso Jejunal tube positioned by specialist
> nurse under radiological guidance. Awaiting radiological
> report before feeding can begin.

Tuesday 10th February

The nights are long.
Nurses tick the minutes
on my SATs chart,
count my breaths,
install the overbearing grip
of a blood pressure cuff.
For £2 I watch TV,
try to get tired enough
to lose consciousness.

> Blood results: NB 118g/l – MCV 86 – WBC 5.7 x10^9/L
> – Neuts 3.7 x10^9/L – Lymph 1.5 x10^9/L

Wednesday 11th February

I see The Consultant twice weekly,
a tall man with a round stomach.
He wears a suit with a quirky tie
and isn't good at washing his hands.
His laugh is springy and fake,
the professional equivalent
of a kid's bouncy ball.

> Continue regime as prescribed.

Thursday 12th February

My 17th birthday.
I unwrap presents
meant for another self.
A laser printer for uni,
a sewing kit,
makeup.
I begin vomiting
after moving
too violently
as the ward sings
Happy Birthday,
carrying a cake
made of blue
paper towels.
In this life
I have just turned one,
my body a regressing flip book.

Patient has persisting nausea and dizziness, very low blood pressure and remains pale.

Sunday 15th February

I can tell if the needle is in a vein
because the pain is different –
dull in empty tissue,
sharp when harvestable.
On his eighth try, I ask The Consultant
if I can have a go.

Full blood count, clotting, Urea and Electrolytes, Liver Function Test, Thyroid Function tests all normal except for expected neutropenia, anaemia and elevated infection markers consistent with pyrexia.

Tuesday 17th February

For nine days, my body has been achieving the "physically impossible",
rejecting calories from past my stomach. For nine days I've vomited,

for nine days The Consultant said it wasn't feed, for nine days he ordered
the nurses to ignore my writhing. It shouldn't be possible
to shut your patient down like a building. He says blood
in vomit is normal. It takes Stella, a junior, to order an x-ray:
"It's possible. I've read about it in textbooks."

> In the early morning patient deteriorated suddenly,
> Blood pressure only found on 72/36, 1 litre of normal
> saline pushed into 2x venous access, patient improved.
>
> There is significant evidence to support a probable
> diagnosis of Intestinal Failure.

Wednesday 18th February

The play leader is one of three professionals I trust.
He hands me another set of colouring books,
talks about the kid who can't be left alone:
how he raises the mechanical bed two metres up
and keeps jumping off from boredom.
This afternoon, we're using the badge maker
and Cath Kidston tissues to make gifts
for my school friends. Normalcy is long gone.

> IV medications rewritten to allow for about 4 hours
> between having Ondansetron and Metoclopramide
> to help prevent nausea and sickness. Urine needed
> for cultures, bloods and new cannular.

Thursday 19th February

My bowel is coiled, a snake resting in my abdomen.
The doctors test its reflexes, see if it will strike
after being antagonised. There is no response.
The zookeepers glance at each other,
bury their faces into clipboards.

> Preliminary results of Sphincter Electromyography
> suggest significant issues. Hannah's muscle motility
> in the intestinal tract is the opposite to what we
> would expect.

Saturday 21st February

I'm holding a memorial service:
I remember hot Ribena on bitter afternoons.
I remember fish fingers in buttered baps.
I remember baked beans as the enemy of Breakfast.

Patient asked about her suitability for a Gastric electrical stimulator. This is not something routinely offered in the UK and has proven to be of very little long-term benefit. She continues to be nil by mouth, getting all nutrition via naso jejunal tube.

Monday 23rd February

A flexible metal probe is passed up my nose
and down my oesophagus. It's marked at staggered points,
a thermometer of how high gastric acid travels
whilst I'm sleeping. There is a plastic box
attached to the wire, a Blackbox,
only interpreted after catastrophe,
contructed to outlast its user.

Oesophageal pH monitor placed to be worn for 24 hours. Initial results indicate advanced symptoms and non-tolerance of oral diet or hydration.

Tuesday 24th February

Forgetting how to answer a question
is like routing around in your bag,
trying to find the ticket you bought,
definitely bought, to show the conductor.
The Consultant orders a brain scan.

Urgent MRI request: to query either stroke or bleed.

Wednesday 25th February

My body is a word search
in which I've found three conditions.
The Consultant says he's never seen them before,

More of a sudoku. We sit close
Dr Stella and I,
my room turned puzzle corner.

> Ongoing diagnostic hypotheses' include Ehlers Danlos
> Syndrome, Intestinal Failure, POTs syndrome &
> Hypovolemia

Thursday 26th February

I've been off my medication for twenty-four hours
for an accurate barium x-ray swallow.
The pain is water, pushing through the floodgates of my nose,
my head, puddling in my lungs. The registrar grabs my shoulders,
turns the oxygen valve up to four litres. "Hannah, you're having
a panic attack from pain. I've read your notes,
and will give you your meds, this is as much of a test result
as we need. Take some nice big breaths for me,
it's okay, you're okay, the medicine will help."
She glances in the vomit bowl streaked with blood,
anyone who has seen a Casualty episode knows
quite how much. "He can't just leave you like this.
There's no safe way for you to stay as you are."

> Request for Consultant to come in and review
> patient. Significant oesophageal trauma due to retching
> due to Ondansetron cessation. Immediate re-starting of
> all medications and benzodiazepine prescribed in the
> hope her muscles stop contracting and she can
> get some much-deserved sleep.

Friday 27th February

Bemused, the House Officer says:
"You need to tell him he's a very clever man,
then ask him to refer you to someone else."

> Patient in good spirits. Observations remain amber, and
> vitals remain shaky. Physical examination reveals possible
> torn muscles due to extended periods of vomiting.

Monday 2nd March

The Consultant arrives on the ward, with a smile sewn on
like a scouting badge. He's spoken to the specialist centre
who have referred me for testing. "So" he says "we'll see
if all of this is anything much at all." The fan hisses,
my mother's neutral expression turns more dark.
"We will," I say. "We will," says Mum.

> Referred for specialist opinion at 1 of 2 specialist units
> for Intestinal Failure in the country.

Tuesday 3rd March

Sometimes I wish to be powder –
to move without pain in the breeze,
to have a small chance at arriving home.

> Intravenous bolus Ranitidine is causing Hannah
> headaches and double vision. I have changed the
> prescription so it can be used via a syringe driver, 30mls/
> 30 minutes.

Wednesday 4th March

I tell a nurse that I'm hungry,
that tube feeding hurts
and I miss the experience of food.
She says: "I'm a vegetarian,
I completely understand missing out."

> She has worsening oropharyngeal choking sensations and
> has been referred to Speech and Language Therapy.

Thursday 5th March

Today I found out I've won
my first poetry competition.
The email says I must reply,
otherwise the trophy will be given
to second place. Nurse [Redacted]
lets me use the computer with a walking desk,

which breaks data protection policy.
Mum logs into my emails, looking over
her shoulder periodically as if security
are waiting, and this happiness is a trap.

> Hannah has won a little Amnesty International Poetry Competition. She seems very happy, but her tachycardia has still been spiking, this would exclude it being caused by anxiety. I have chased her cardiology referral.

Saturday 7th March

I've become an envelope folded over state secrets.
A doctor reads my x-rays. He does not explain them.
Machines do not solve enigma alone.

> 2nd opinion of X-ray sought due to possible malformation seen in abdomen.

Monday 9th March

My friend comes up to the ward.
Our bodies sway back and forth
like saplings unable to support each other.

> I have written to my pharmacological colleagues to ask if intravenous preparations of medications can be taken jejunally if no solution is on the market.

Tuesday 10th March

The MRI scanner has such a powerful magnet
you get changed two rooms away,
leave bobbles and bras in a cubicle and wear a gown.

In India, this machine killed a man
when an oxygen cannister took flight as if possessed,
towards him, crushing his skull.

The radiologist secures my head in a frame
with a mirror designed for toddlers.
She speaks to me through the microphone

and begins the scan. I hold my breath
waiting for my body to produce
a spontaneous cannister.

Patient refused sedation we offered by citing the 'over-hang' it has on her for the next few days.

Wednesday 11th March

The Children's hospital have a policy
not to operate on over sixteens,
while the Adult hospital refuses to operate
on under eighteens. Age seventeen I'm stuck
in my cage of illness,
while two departments with bolt cutters
argue over who should let me out.

I have written to both the Children's and Adult's hospital Managing Directors to try and resolve this dispute in policy.

Friday 13th March

Slices of my body the thickness of a bible page
appear on the computer system.
The Radiologist doesn't understand
what he's seeing, forwards my scans
to the specialist centre.

We have increased cardiac medications, but this has produced black stools suggestive of melena. We have now halved the dose and will observe.

Saturday 14th March

I can't impeach the system of mealtimes,
but try to distract myself as food arrives on the ward.
The only channel available is the fourth one,
showing Come Dine With Me *reruns.*

Hannah has suffered a viral-like illness and following this has developed a deterioration in her symptoms.

Her blood pressure remains in order of 80/40 but her heart rate is still running between 100 and 150 beats per minute.

Sunday 15th March

Home. The word is an insect,
that scuttles from my tongue.
The Consultant shrugs, medical terms spill
from his lips like shaving foam; mess spurting,
a tap with no urgency or pressure.

I have reassured Hannah today that her echocardiogram scan was normal, with only mild mitral regurgitation and mild tricuspid regurgitation.

Monday 16th March

The intravenous team use a scalpel five times,
to try and find a vein. They slip out of view
as they cut them, naughty children avoiding
their grandfather's slipper. I refuse sedation,
learn regret is red and drips onto pillows.

They thread plastic through a map of veins,
from elbow to shoulder. Sterile dressing,
clots wiped from bed, floppy jellyfish
reproducing outside my faulty ecosystem.

Successful midline placement on the 6th attempt. Continued trying at patient's request because she understands the escalation of care a different line would require. Venous access waning, we may need to consider ankle midline or arterial access centrally if this is to continue.

Tuesday 17th March

The Specialist Centre writes back to The Consultant.
The tests are spray paint
highlighting my potholes,
making obvious issues unavoidable.

Cardiac medication main limiting symptoms include worsening hypotension, presyncope and syncope.

Wednesday 18th March

Today I used a wheelchair for the first time –
gained the identity of tracing paper.
A simple film written on, then discarded,
a quick sketch of something, someone.

Hannah's reflexes are absent throughout all joints. Muscle tone reduced in upper limbs. Referred to neurophysiology.

Friday 20th March

I watch the eclipse from a tall rectangular window.
I'm too sick to go outside and watch it with the play leader
who is standing outside in his rally helmet.

It's cloudy, but all the kids are given a certificate –
even those on ICU, unconscious.
A nurse comforts a crying mother.

"Most kids born today will live for a century."
A health care assistant bites her lip,
the kid's father scuffing his shoes against the skirting board.

Hannah's abdomen is soft on palpation, but she is still struggling with continence issues. I have prescribed the maximum adult dose of laxative and am at a loss. I suggest we continue with the current regime and wait for any outcome.

Saturday 21st March

Retrospect makes you realise
how much can be lost
despite keeping all of your possessions.

Hannah has had quite a bad dislocation of her knee and has had previous issues with her Anterior Cruciate Ligament.

Sunday 22nd March

I played bingo with the playleader today.
We pranked a cleaner with my prize,
a robotic fish she believed was real.
She was very concerned for its welfare,
in a clear plastic bag. I look around
my isolation room, and confidently
say: "I know how it feels."

Hannah has asked that I research endo flip and post pyloric Botox. My understanding of these procedures are limited, and though they may be appropriate in her disease I'm not convinced they would improve her outcome.

Monday 23rd March

I ask The Consultant four times
if he's ever done this operation before.
He eventually says no, tries to explain
how it will be done.

He will liberate my stomach acid
but burn my abdomen.
He says I must trust him, he hasn't earned
that many stars on his behaviour chart.

His anger escalates to hurdles,
my doubt an athlete tripping over them.

Hannah has consented to the procedure; I will consult with a Consultant I know in Australia who has done numerous G-J Tubes and will offer helpful advice.

Tuesday 24th March

Parents line the corridors, wood
rotting from the inside out.
We're trying chemo one last time.
This mum, immaculate makeup,
wishes she could smudge foundation

over the tumour,
take her child home.

She's got a head injury.
We don't know if,
we aren't sure if
we
we don't know if –
Outside A&E this dad circles,
stuck on a roundabout in shock.

They're ventilating him, please come.
Outside HDU this new mum phones her mum,
panic demolishing her features.

These people,
stunned paintings
walking corridors.

> I have encouraged Hannah to mobilise around the hospital in the hope of stimulating her bowel.

Thursday 26th March

"You seem in good spirits," my friend says.
She keeps her eyes level, swallowing nervously,
watching me intently, like she can see my brain
without Scanner. She leaves after 3 hours.
In the evening, I embroider my smile,
hiding blood and scabs with lip gloss.

> Hannah has been quite emotional outside of her friends visiting. She is keen to continue her jejunal feeding to see if she can get enough time (8 hours) off so that she won't need to carry her feed pump around at school. Given the danger of jejunal feeding at fast rates this is unlikely, but she wants to try.

Saturday 28th March

The radiographer is a building inspector,

unhappy with the integrity of my body.
she declares my body structurally unsound.

> Hannah's muscle motility in the intestinal tract is the opposite to what we would expect. This has flicked the tube in her bowel up to her stomach, rather than being progressed further into the jejunum. Hannah had a replacement NJ placed this morning.

Sunday 29th March

Fainting is breathing whilst submerged in syrup,
the heft of sugar, the slow motion of stickiness.

> Hannah's blood pressure has remained low and hasn't rallied for some time. While they are faints, they do have the hallmarks of a more severe collapse.

Monday 30th March

The doctors pass a second tube up my nose,
down my throat, and into my stomach.
My body can't process saliva any more.
I have two feeding lines across my cheeks,
a house with two downspouts.

> Naso gastric tube passed to drain stomach bile and saliva. Retching has stopped since due to stomach contents being drained freely.

Tuesday 31st March

I feel the bulge then pop of propofol as it bursts my vein
consciousness melting, meat dripping as it defrosts.
I shout "ow! Stop, please st—"

> Procedure went as planned, although re-cannulation was required upon intubation. Patient is on 2l oxygen until 9pm when it will be reassessed. Limited trauma. Recovery should be quick.

Wednesday 1st April

Just as a balloon cannot control breath
I can't control weight, kilos keep escaping like air.

> The Specialist Centre has written to advise that we stop
> all Fybogel as it is a bulking agent which is likely to cause
> obstruction in someone with Hannah's probable diagnosis.

Thursday 2nd April

"I'm sick of my bleep going off and it's you" my nurse Denise says,
so she admits to altering my observations on the iPad.
She rolls her eyes an hour later when I faint, insists I'm just anxious.
She won't give me medication,
is pleased when I start vomiting.
She knows I enjoy crafting
and smiles as my stomach tie-dyes my top yellow.

[No entry recorded]

Friday 3rd April

I put in a formal complaint.
The other nurses believe me
but can't say anything
because of union regulation.
The Matron checks my notes,
there is no signature next to last night's medication.
She invites Denise into my cubicle.
She says, "I do not recall events as you describe them".
The Matron nods.

> Patient is speaking with senior management about a
> possible incident last night. It has been requested that we
> discuss her care during the grand round meeting but do
> not visit her bedside today as she is very tired.

Saturday 4th April

I want to rip off my skin like tear-able stage clothing,
but can't. My body disgustingly full

like a hoarder's home.
No amount of showering can fix insides,
or the past.

[The unrecordable thing wasn't written down]

Sunday 5th April

Teach me how to pray to my flesh,
worship every breath,
wear myself like a Cathedral again.

Hannah seems highly distressed and unwilling for staff members to help her. I have phoned psychology and asked them to review her this afternoon. It could be that the gravity of her physical health situation is hitting home.

Monday 6th April

I've been keeping to myself –
treating my memories as flowers
pressing them between pages of a medical dictionary,
in a prolonged funeral of childhood.

Hannah has been sleeping during the day and staying awake most of the night. She seems unsettled. I have swapped her nurse tonight in case the ongoing complaint is making her uncomfortable.

Tuesday 7th April

I wish to mould fat like clay,
fill this in. My thigh gap is everything

I stand against.	*It sags, my skin*
under	*inflated*
I wish to	*refill, this body*
made of	*wax,*
evaporating	*into nothing.*
Calories	*burnt once,*
and gone	*forever.*

28

Hannah has requested that her Feed Vital 1.5 be increased to 35mls/hr, meaning per hour she is connected she gets 47 calories.

Thursday 9th April

Today I was trained
to insert a needle
like a candle wick into my fat.

Hannah has been successfully trained in hand hygiene and subcutaneous drug delivery.

Friday 10th April

Stella says: "It's quite likely you'll never eat again"
as easily as suggesting a blood culture.
She tells me during a visit with my grandparents,
who don't understand anything past
her white coat. I say "Okay".
Crows whistling through my teeth,
grief inaudible.

Long term prognosis conversation began to little reaction. Unsure she understands the bigger picture.

Saturday 11th April

My brother turns fourteen today.
Mum has gone home.
It isn't just blood and electrolytes I'm losing —
it's a whole forest being taken
by a thing as simple as a chainsaw.

L is no longer present at bedside, Hannah appears on edge.

Sunday 12th April

Nurse Steph gives me three intramuscular injections.
One in my buttock, and another in each arm.
She places my shoes on my feet, as delicately

as glass slippers. "You take it easy.
Your vitals aren't exactly normal."

B12, Lorazepam and Metoclopramide all delivered by intramuscular injection. Watch for any paralysis in the left leg, as there were no sites which aren't hardened inside usual areas.

Monday 13th April

My fifth audition for the SAW franchise
arrives, as the scalpel nears my arm
I watch. I don't flinch,
and maybe that's the reason
I'm trapped here, not given the part.
I thank the production crew, they smile
explaining my new prosthetic makeup,
a midline peaking from my arm like an apple.

Procedure was successful with delicate positioning.

Tuesday 14th April

School sent me an email.
They're delaying my exams,
and though I agree
it doesn't stop me from feeling
like a dog leashed to this drip stand,
unable to go home.

Cardiology diagnosis of Hypovolemia. Advised we give 3 litres of fluid per day infinitum, increasing blood volume.

Wednesday 15th April

I saw my maths teacher today –
walking into clinic with his daughters.
He said: "Hi, how are you?"
but I couldn't place him,
his name rising like bread
in my consciousness.

Discussed and agreed Genetic Testing risk/benefits. Advised her that waiting lists are 1y plus, & the NHS doesn't offer full genomic evaluation for 'adults' (age 16+).

Thursday 16th April

Today my body manages the transition
from IV to NJ Tube medications.
These take three hours at a ml per 60 seconds.
My gut should be a motorway,
but instead there's green signs
reading Twenty's Plenty.

I have transferred all medication from IV to NJ. In case of an issue IV medications still as prescribed.

Friday 17th April

My friends have come down on the train.
They know more about this city than I do.
They watch my body, mentally drawing
criminal chalk lines around my changed person.
One starts: "You've lost so much weig-um." She shuffles
in her seat. "I mean you're so thin. We'll shop for clothes
when you're home." Another says "Can I hug you?
I'm not going to break any of the machines or hurt you, am I?"
I'm so outside of the world I no longer have emotion.
I wish for the days when we hated each other, to feel
such pointless sadness, to be desperate for a snog
instead of survival.

Ultrasound shows full bladder, patient has no sensation. Advice: toilet every 6h. Watch kidney function. Any decrease indicative of Kidney Damage/Failure (already borderline).

Saturday 18th April

I've mastered the art of crying silently into my pillow,
so I don't wake the baby with an open fracture,
due to get surgery tomorrow.

On ultrasound I can see she isn't getting the signals for a full bladder. I have encouraged her to try and go to the toilet every 6 hours. We are hopeful she can regain the ability to empty her bladder without catheterisation.

Sunday 19th April

The emergency bell has sounded four times in the last hour
despite no one needing help. Eventually, staff check the alarms in all rooms,
and find a grown man hiding in the room of a baby girl.
No one knows how he got in, what he's done.

Due to exceptional circumstances I have not been able to review Hannah in any depth today. She tells me that she has no new presenting complaints.

Monday 20th April

It's a bank holiday –
so volunteers replace the play staff.
They hand me a sudoku
and recommend I read Me Before You.
The main character is disabled,
and in the end kills himself. He dies, made to believe
he is a burden to his girlfriend.
I go back to the sudoku.

No alterations to current care, as I will leave this to her Consultant who now knows her well.

Tuesday 21st April

My body has installed weights in my muscles.
I stay in bed for a full twenty-four hours, my blankets acting as gauze.

Hannah has extreme symptoms of fatigue and I have asked the cardiology and neurology teams to review her.

Wednesday 22nd April

There's no surgeon
to separate my personality from body,
like mould out of a jam jar.

> Cardiology and Neurology conditions are stable but chronic. I have upped her dose of Amitriptyline in the hope she will have a more restful night's sleep.

Thursday 23rd April

Auntie came today. Out of nervousness
she revealed a family secret.
It calcified and fell out onto my bed like a molar.
My mother is reaching out an arm,
for now a crater is
threatening to swallow us.

> Both the patient and I are disappointed that Ivabradine was not tolerated. It helped palpitations but increased the frequency of migraines from once per week to once per day.

Sunday 26th April

Steph checks the corridor before coming in the room.
"You seem sad," she says. I nod.
I feel like snow disappearing into wet ground,
(but I'm not self-righteous enough to say that out loud).
"You're being treated really badly here.
Promise me you'll complain when you're home?
Things have got to change." I nod.

> Patient appears stable and happy. Her blood oxygen percentages drop upon standing, but her plans today mostly involve 'resting'.

Tuesday 28th April

The play leader tells me a story of a girl four doors down.
She threw her pizza across the ward as a Frisbee,

because it only had a single circle of pepperoni.
She's a representative on the hospital food board.

> Hannah has started experiencing increased sensory disturbance in her hands. It started in her fingertips bilaterally and has crept up her hands in the past few days, where it appears to have stopped.

Wednesday 29th April

I forget I shouldn't stand up,
that I need to allow my blood to cool;
let the kettle of my heart click off
at the height of its boil.

> Hannah appeared distressed and disorientated after fainting today. We put her legs on a chair and administered PRN medication for this eventuality and her vitals improved.

Thursday 30th April

"I will make you better by April,"
The Consultant said last November.
I wish to erase those words
like music notes, recompose
that conversation, oh, the expectation.
The hope that today
he'd finally have a full orchestra.

> She has right sided cramping/dystonic movements. I have prescribed Baclofen TDS and will review in 48 hours.

Friday 1st May

Nana came today. She used the photo album
as garden shears – tried to create a gap big enough for chatter.

> Hannah has been troubled by excessive fatigue. The history of her symptoms are not consistent with Chronic Fatigue Syndrome. This is also her view.

Nevertheless, we have discussed strategies recommended for CFS, and repurposed them for her fatigue, as a trial.

Sunday 3rd May

A whole room of people jump
like cutlery on a slammed table.
The Consultant shouts:
"Yes. I've never seen your condition before
but I am perfectly capable!" He storms out.

Patient asked for a second opinion, but I assured her we are consulting with experts in this field.

Tuesday 5th May

I've stayed in bed all day with a migraine.
My head is a dark room developing snapshots,
evidence of past months.

Unfortunately, Hannah has had a series of severe migraine episodes over the past 24 hours, which have been treated with intravenous paracetamol and her usual migraine relief. At Hannah's request of "Can you prescribe some darkness?", we shut her curtains.

Thursday 7th May

I've watched a whole season of Friends in the past
twenty-four hours. The intravenous team opens veins
with a scalpel: incisions carved the shape of apple pips;
little, red mouths in my skin, stitched closed.

Successful procedure.

Saturday 9th May

The doctor scans the ground of my hands,
paces up and down my arms with an ultrasound –
an archaeologist struggling to discover artefacts.

She finds fragments in my left inside elbow,
a glimpse of riches once ravaged by another junior.
She rolls her head around her shoulders, tells me to relax

and slaps my arm. Nothing. She begins scanning my foot –
discovers a tunnel in my left ankle. "Keep very still,"
she says, while installing a joist in the shaft.

She extracts riches of dubious value,
sends them to the lab for appraisal.
She removes the needle,

hands me cotton wool and presses
hard. Clots seal my vault.

> No prominent veins visible due to scarring and
> hypovolemia. Ultrasound was used to trace deep veins
> which are non-palpable. Blood sample drawn.

Sunday 10th May

The ward laughs harder than it has in months.
Parents compare the length of their sausage balloons,
wait for the entertainer to blow his whistle.
The balloons race across the bay,
the owner of the fastest wins an air-filled crown.
There are elements of my mother's smile
if you scratch the air
with phallic balloons.
Her happiness is everywhere,
a lotto tickets uncovered by pennies.
Jackpot.

> Hannah has had a drain fitted in the pit of her stomach
> (pylorus) in the 'Dip in the Pond position'.

Monday 11th May

There are four hospitals in a row,
like terraced houses with an interlinking corridor.
Childrens, Maternity, Eye and Adults.
I sit in the Eye hospital

watch a fake tree not grow. There is such
falsified brightness here, too many LED strips.
When I speak, my past life echoes.

Hannah's stomach secretions remain green/black, suggestive of intermittent blockage. Referred for assessment for bowel washout suitability.

Tuesday 12th May

I've been having dreams in which I'm strangled.
When I research the meaning of this on dreamthesaurus.com
and I'm informed I'm feeling suffocated.
I needn't have asked specialist opinion.

Full barrier nursing undertaken due to neutrophils of 0.5.

Wednesday 13th May

An air bubble the length of a sausage balloon
advances down my IV tubing. I gaze at it.
Flick at it like I've seen the nurses do.
I press my call bell. No response.
I clamp the tubing when air is just centimetres
from my blood. My nurse comes in.
Inspects it. "Oh dear," she whispers.
Following it down to the clamp.
She sighs.
She doesn't say an air embolus
has a rate of fifty per cent survival.
"Can we keep this between us?" she asks.

Hannah remains stable. I have chased her referrals to other services, specifically neuro at the Tertiary Centre.

Thursday 14th May

The Consultant tells me to prepare this body
for a slow demolition of lost function.

We informed Hannah of her probable diagnosis from the Specialist Centre. She has an appointment in outpatients soon with Professor McNulty, who provided this diagnosis. She seems to be digesting the news.

Friday 15th May

Stella asks if The Consultant came yesterday,
if I know my condition is incurable.
I nod, she says she's set up Google alerts on her phone,
that she hopes one day we both hear bells.

Discussed the probable diagnosis with Hannah, who mentioned she has been having neck pain of late at the atlanto-axial level. She is extremely hypermobile in this area. I advised that if she wishes to pursue this further, she will need a neurosurgical opinion. However, my understanding is that in the UK experts in this field advise against any invasive surgical intervention.

Saturday 16th May

Today was the awards ceremony for the Amnesty International competition in
London. I can't go, but was surprised in the corridor by the chief executive of the
hospital, holding my poem. The photos are: Hospital grey/ beige with flecks of
green and red in the lino/ NHS uniforms/ Staff I've never met/ smiling in
unison. The Play Leader tells me he bought the frame himself. It's John Lewis.
I am worthy of celebration.

Nowhere's Citizen

State decision looms,
muttered opinion spread –
"Nowhere!" is the answer
pinned to my head.

You hum "Don't belong here"
my face again scanned,
worded cufflinks hold me
trapped to the land.

Deportation disallowed –
I can't stay or go,
all my protest silenced,
again I'm told "No!"

No choice before me,
mattress a concrete crack,
the tag 'nowhere's citizen'
branded to my back.

Tethered to the country,
through which I cannot roam,
no passport handed to me,
freedom on loan.

Listen to my voice,
I'm living here now,
make my future brighter –
together we know how!

Sunday 17th May

I get an x-ray of a bowel perforation,
and the immediate finding is I'm wearing an underwired bra.
For moments, teen embarrassment supersedes mortality,
the massive pocket of air creaking
beneath the skin of my abdomen.

> Hannah has a pneumoperitoneum revealed in x-ray. This
> will be managed conservatively in conjunction with our
> surgical colleagues.

Monday 18th May

Possible side effects include:
Vomiting
Visual impairment
Syncope
Peripheral Vascular Disease
Paraesthesia
Heart Failure
Dyspnoea
Abdominal Discomfort (pain)
Moderate Abdominal Discomfort (PAIN)
Hallucinations
Atrioventricular Block
Bronchospasm

I ask The Consultant how likely these are.
He says "I don't know". For all the science involved,
medicine isn't certain.

> I've started Hannah on Propranolol and we have
> discussed risk/benefit analysis. She is happy to proceed.

Wednesday 20th May

The Heart MRI opens my chest like a gated garden,
shows the doctors the paths of my arteries,
the automatic doors of my valves and oxygen.

Heart MRI is reassuringly normal. T-Wave inversion is exceptionally rare in her age, gender and ethnicity, so it is likely to be caused by her underlying disease.

Thursday 21st May

The neurologist says I'm under observation for abnormalities the next five days.
He tells me: it often snows inside my brain, but he can't trace the weather system.

Hannah has had a continuation of her neurological symptoms, in particular paraesthesia in her hands and feet.

Friday 22nd May

He tells me: you've protected
your memories with locks,
but forgot about the existence
of bolt cutters.

We have commenced Fludrocortisone and increased Amitriptyline and Baclofen dosage rates.

Saturday 23rd May

He tells me: the cables
between organs have snapped,
replacement wiring not available.
I am vintage. Nothing to be done.

We have contacted Hannah's local Clinical Commissioning group to request a meeting before her community discharge, and the possibility of future Continuing Care input.

Sunday 24th May

He tells me: your lefts and rights
have become indistinguishable.
He suggests a tattoo could help.

We have tested Hannah for Mast Cell Activation Syndrome. Results are unclear. However, all airborne allergen blood tests have come back positive.

Tuesday 26th May

I talk to The Consultant about the feed pumped into my bowel.
I ask him if there's a vegetarian version.
He rolls his eyes, "Why is it always the girls?
What do you love more – animals or life itself?"

Hannah and the team discussed her current feeding regime but decided to keep it the same.

Wednesday 27th May

My stomach takes forty-eight hours to empty.
If I drink apple juice I brew my own cider.
Milk solidifies into curds.
Butter dissolves into tissue like toast.
Rice buds from shoots.
Eggs incubate and hatch.

Second Barium Follow-through shows continued dysmotility and only minor improvement – although this is likely due to Hannah's bizarre reaction to Buscopan in that it gives her extreme abdominal cramping, thus pushing the Barium through at an accelerated rate.

Thursday 28th May

I'm alone in the bay, so the entertainer drops her act
as soon as the door is closed. "I can't stand this place.
I'm quitting. No joke – I've applied to join the circus as my get out."

The Medicine Management Team reviewed Hannah's prescriptions. Unfortunately, they weren't able to cut the list. All are of high clinical need.

Saturday 30th May

It looks like cola has exploded over my arms;
the bubbles settling on skin
as they do in plastic bottles.
I'm fed the equivalent of cola,
for those unable to sip,
scars from over-cannulations.
They call them tiny straws
instead, I see butterfly tongues.

We cannot prescribe the contraceptive pill to help with anaemia by prevention of periods. I contacted the gynae service at the women's hospital who were too busy for a consult & suggested she phone her GP to ask that a script be sent out in the post.

Sunday 31st May

The body is a Jack O'Lantern,
attracting unhelpful moths.
My face is calved and rotting,
flame soon to retract into smoke.
All insides have disappeared,
nobody saw the vandals.
They came in the night
and took me with ladles.

I have prescribed Hannah antibiotics as her most recent bloods suggest infection. This is likely due to a mysterious bite which appeared a few days ago, and has since become infected.

Tuesday 2nd June

I keep tending to my fire.
I've long run out of wood.
I blow on embers.
I need the heat of it to keep me here.
Away from hypothermia.

Psychology assessment confirms Hannah having difficulty understanding the long-term repercussions of her diagnosis. She has no outpatient mental health input, due to her age and lack of suicidal ideation.

Wednesday 3rd June

Of late, my friends believe
I'm a country they need jabs
and a passport for.

Hannah was wearing shoes today, and I noticed that her right one was extremely scuffed. I asked her how long she has been dragging her foot. She says she isn't sure. I have updated neurology.

Friday 5th June

This is the second time junior doctors
have changed rotation during my stay here.
Stella is now stationed in the Bone Marrow unit,
but says she'll visit if she can. The newbies arrive
like suspect packages awaiting my assessment.
It'll take weeks to determine their worth.

Patient appears tired but comfortable. Sats 96%, resps 11 and pulse 119.

Saturday 6th June

Opposite the ward is the county CAMHS unit.
A girl sits rocking, smiling while talking to the air.
I've tried to get her attention for five months.
She has never looked at me, her sari glinting.
As a magpie I can't help but peck at the glass.

Hannah expressed a wish to go outside before her surgery. We stopped all infusions and provided a wheelchair. She appears happy.

Sunday 7th June

The playleader came into hospital today
on his second week of paternity leave
holding his new born up to the window.
I feel as a stadium must, as its roof opens for the first time.
How can a building so dark contain stars?

Both Children's and Adults services input upon discharge due to her need for an Educational Health Care plan, returning to education in September.

Monday 8th June

The complex medicine team come on the ward,
close the curtain around me.
Ask when did your symptoms start?
and I realise I've had symptoms my whole life:
that I should re-examine old photographs like x-rays,
mount them onto the light boxes on the wall.
I re-watch my baby video, containing
a missing person. The video cuts out,
fuzzes for seconds and lands on an episode of Jeremy Kyle:
lie detector,
DNA, fall out,
the effort behind a shouting match.

Advanced history taken including family, began to be symptomatic at 6 months old, seen at Magdalena Hall in 2007 and discharged back to local care. Reassured patient that even if we had known of her condition at a young age her treatment would be the same.

Wednesday 10th June

Before discharge sit exams in myself.
Playing Hospital, soon to bring home.

Hannah has been signed off with her training on handwashing, enteral feeding, medication management and subcutaneous needle insertion, and subcutaneous fluids.

Thursday 11th June

Today the ward drains backed up,
looked like brown tinned beans
emerging across the ward.
They relocated us,
while jackhammers take up the floor.
A secret city of pipes is revealed,
rusted beneath our hospital beds,
each half a tonne.

Transferred to ward M2 overnight due to issue with drainage on the ward. Regime remains the same.

Friday 12th June

I am a princess
locked in the tower
of my skeleton.

I have ordered Hannah's medical equipment for discharge. 2 Nutricia Flocare infinity pumps, 1 subcutaneous syringe driver, 1 Alaris plus Enteral syringe driver, 1 hospital bed, 1 manual wheelchair and 1 4-pronged drip stand. There are other needs but I have written to her local Occupational Therapist.

Saturday 13th June

I'm sat outside. Kids aren't allowed out here.
There are needles in the Wendy House,
left by last night's occupants.

Hannah's blood type is B+ in those significant antibodies, haemoglobin is 13.2, normal though slightly low white cell count, normal platelets, U and E's identified slightly low potassium which we are rectifying. She is cleared and ready for surgery.

Sunday 14th June

Nurses specialise in the butterfly knock –
the official 'I'm coming in anyway' notification.
Today I was caught in tears, my face a geezer.
She held my hand, I know you're scared but life is a maze –
your body has sent you in the wrong direction,
but your personality, your drive, that's your way out.

> Attempted to discuss the impact on her body image
> this operation will have. Hannah was very defensive and
> deflective, just saying she wants to get home. This psyche
> is understandable.

Monday 15th June

Today, Donald Trump announces he is running for US President;
the remains of a two-thousand-year-old 'Sleeping Beauty' have been found,
and I awake from surgery with a trunk permanently installed in my abdomen.

> A few anaesthetic difficulties but procedure itself was
> successful.

Tuesday 16th June

I have bruises along my jaw like fairy steps.
The Surgeon said I was "a tricky one" to intubate.
On paper, everything is well.

> Xray taken of abdomen showing correct tube
> placement. Feeding commenced at 5mls an hour with
> no vomiting. We hope to increase this by 5mls every
> 6 hours, and have Hannah gain some weight before
> discharge.

Wednesday 17th June

I wouldn't feel guilty if someone burgled my home,
but illness has burgled my expected future,
and guilt is my shadow even with eyes closed.
I wish illness and I could be separate entities –
then I'd have someone else to blame for this condition.

IV iron infusion running over 6 hours, no significant allergic response. IV saline + 200mmol Potassium running after and glucose prescribed for overnight.

Thursday 18th June

It's three days post operation.
When I sit up my eyes tunnel
candle flame losing oxygen.

We have prescribed Hannah some Morphine 5mg–5ml. Although not ideal due to its effects on the gut. Both mum and nurses caught her as she fainted attempting to get out of bed. These were not accompanied by the usual tachycardia and appeared to be caused by pain. She is now asleep.

Friday 19th June

For a two-year-old, six months is a quarter of a lifetime.
For me, this admission has been a thirty secondth
of my lived experience. Leaving the shuttle of my bed
is such an undertaking, it's become a spacewalk.

Hives and vomiting allergic response to Flucloxacillin. Noted as sensitivity, only to be used if she is at risk of sepsis and benefits outweigh risk.

Sunday 21st June

School friends will remember me like Christmas decorations at the end of term.
Cobwebs plaiting the walls like friendship bracelets.

Patient appears uncomfortable yet stable. Her oxygen percentages are having dips but she quickly recovers. She has significant bruising around the site of her surgery, but upon surgical review they detailed their struggle with her tight muscles due to her disease, so this is to be expected.

Monday 22nd June

I try to explain to The Consultant
that I'm scared of the dreams I'm having.
Hauntings of daytime repackaged.
He says I've nothing, nobody
to be afraid of.

> Patient described possible night terrors. No nurses have witnessed these, and I am unsure if they are as traumatic as she describes. Psychology couldn't attend today, but I will ask for a review before discharge.

Tuesday 23rd June

I lost a kilo this week
my body reverse ghosting,
coming back from translucency.

> <1 kilo weight loss. Reassuring that procedure was successful, and Hannah appears to be tolerating the feed medically speaking.

Wednesday 24th June

Today I've had a discharge meeting.
The Consultant says I can go home
once recovered from my operation.
My muscles unfurl like ribbon, ready.
The Consultant leaves. My new District Nurse
says "What is actually wrong with you?"
And my muscles regain their corseted structure.

> Discharge meeting occurred. Explained complex nature of Hannah's conditions and high nursing needs. Handed on the order codes for Hannah's disposable equipment and offered advice to District Nurse level of input needed.

Thursday 25th June

One of my friends graduates today
so I watch my phone like an expectant animal.
Stroking the case, I wait for the painful.

Oddly, Hannah's platelets appear low. I have ordered repeat blood tests and arranged a possible transfusion. Patient says abdominal pain is unbearable, and abdominal x-rays show significant blockage. I have prescribed above usual prescribable amounts of laxative to her, with full consent, as this appears to be the only thing that works for her. Linaclotide, Prucalopride, Picolax, and both micro and macro enemas, have no effect. Benefit outweighs risk.

Friday 26th June

I take my first shower in weeks –
remove my earrings, my watch
and realise I can't take out my permanent
silicone tubes.
I try to reduce my panic
but fish can't control the waves
they travel in. I wash around
the medical, press gently on the bruises.
Iodine and blood brown puddles.

Hannah asked if the ward had any hair straighteners. While we don't, I feel it is a sign of progress that she wants to do such a thing. She is still swollen, but the tube itself is patent and intact. The wound has no signs of infection and although taking its time to heal (likely due to her EDS), it is showing progress.

Saturday 27th June

Today is neuro clinic. Kids with scars on their head
like apples only bitten with the upper jaw.
Death is close in any kind of museum.

Referred to UCL as an outpatient for Amyloidosis testing and hopefully genetic specialists in the coming months. Continues to no longer have reflexes and issues with sensation, irreversible and connected to disease progression.

Sunday 28th June

It's been two days since the pain dulled,
trailed off like a pen out of ink
and I've started building a new self.
I put on eyeliner for the first time since being here.
The Consultant is finishing ward round.

Patient appears alert and happy. Stood without assistance, applying some makeup. She advised us that although her Chronic symptoms are still painful, her acute surgical pain and complications are no longer a problem. I have sent a script to pharmacy for 2 weeks of medications to be arranged for her discharge.

Monday 29th June

I've re-written myself in here,
nervousness around home means I'm institutionalised.
I soon get over the fact.
Home doesn't have plastic pillows.

Confirmed Diagnosis within Discharge Summary: Pernicious Anaemia. Chronic B12, Potassium and Magnesium deficiencies. Sensio-neural deafness. Generalised Dysmotility (primarily gastrointestinal, but also noted by ENT that fluid in ears doesn't drain as expected). Autonomic Dysfunction. Intestinal Failure. Night terrors. Persistent Tachycardia. T-Wave inversion. Ehlers Danlos Syndrome. Cyclical Neutropenia. Hemiplegic Migraine. Newly occurring Asthma caused by disease progression.

Questions for GP to consider upon discharge: She has a probable overarching diagnosis of Mitochondrial

Disease, and metabolic panels show changes. Considering the speed of deterioration it is appropriate for her to join the Palliative Care Register.

Tuesday 30th June

In these six months,
the ward has become a garden –

relatives sit in daisy chains
around the beds of sick children.

Most days, I follow fairy steps along to the pond
which the nurses have covered using a grate.

There is a field of wildflowers which grows at the same rate
as hair follicles from my bald patch.

Once, I stumbled upon a parliament of crows
who were soon to begin a post-mortem.

Finally, doctors feel my body has earned the key
to its own front garden.

Before leaving, I throw everything on a bonfire
the kids from Renal were using to roast marshmallows.

Mum lays out her belongings
in two piles, brings home with her:

three t-shirts and a singular photo
I keep on the mantelpiece of my chest

as a threat to the body,
a reminder of where I'll go back to.

After Care

A Blue Jug of Daffodils

I'm reminded my stature is getting increasingly short
when my brother skips uni and comes home.
I'm told percentile projections aren't a good
indication, but three inches of me is dead.
I've taken cuttings from the banking flowered
with bulbs. The petals are damp, white,

have the face of my low blood pressure, sweaty white
on the border of everything, when time is short.
Life today is living inside a flower.
It's knowing that Nursing Homes
don't take under fifties, as if the dead
can never start their dying young. *Good*

is all my doctor says, and when *Good*
is all he can say, my body drains to white,
skeleton pushed against skin. *Dead*
Beautiful my dad says without meaning both words. Short
of money, but my body is the only home
I'll ever have; unlike flowers

I have no bulb to resurrect. Life is flowers
gone to seed. Life is cutting something good
to put it on the windowsill and die at home.
Every room is painted off-white
once you're diagnosed. Today I wear my short
floral tea dress. It's the one I'll wear when dead.

My mother says it's the kindest thing – for the dead
to have planned. She purchases flowers
every time I get home from hospital, short
of a card saying I was lucky, that good
health is something we can wish upon, like white
Christmases, lottery wins, or dream homes.

I always believed home is where the heart is, but home
is your heart; without the body we're dead
stems in vases. My face is linen white
eyelids fluttering in and out of consciousness, flower
petals closing in the evening and following the good
sun. I realise how bright, dark then short

the days are. Home is a good,
safe place. Flower roots turn white
shortly before death.

Comorbidity Isn't Death

It's a body surprised
by its tolerance.
A tomato seed fallen
from the waste pipe
of the 7:34 train. Watered
by the same leak –
growing from urine,
growing from excess.
The same train arriving,
the same passengers
unknowingly keeping
this tiny plant alive.

Creation

for Lydia

Day One: *Light and Dark*

I'm restrained until it isn't light any more.
Counting the ceiling tiles, watching shadows leer
away from the sun. They ask if I have any metal
in my body. I mention the Kit Kat wrapper
my mother found in my stool at six months old.

Day Two: *The Seas and Clouds*

I cry until my face isn't wet any more.
Stagnant water buildings in my oesophagus.
The grey hat gathers my sickness to be weighed
and measured. The catheter collects my liquids
like a weather station. The tide lingers,
the sickness bobbing alongside in a tiny raft.

Day Three: *Land, Plants and Trees*

I lower the bed until it isn't a summit any more,
climb it in millimetres, caught from falling
by bedrails, a guidewire.
I rest against the tree of a pillow,
catch my breath before it's caught
on my behalf. I check my fall risk socks
for studs, tiny suckers to help this work.

Day Four: *Moon, Sun and Stars*

I scream until I know they're not listening any more.
My mother isn't allowed here unless I start to die
and today that seems a fair price. The moon glows
from behind the one-ply cotton curtains. My parents
wait inside the glow, and I arrive inside the sun.

Day Five: *Birds and Fish*

I beg until I shouldn't any more, until the drowning pauses
and god creates gills. I want my mother's night clothes,
milk-stained dress placed at the bottom
of my cot so I can still smell her and sleep through.

Day Six: *Man and Animals*

I cough until my stitches can't any more.
My exhale sounding like a deer in distress.
The doctors say it's my decision when to go home.
Home is a chocolate they'll place on my pillow,
hurry, hurry away now from painkillers.

Day Seven: *Rest*

I paint my nails until the layers won't dry any more.
Others insist that this, all of this, is good.

Dancing with a Doctor

She tried to dance with me until I fainted.
I saw it then, the medical flickering,
making her face a lighter. She remembers
my body as a candlestick, that I'm nearly spent

and she tries to scrape the wax of me
off the windowsill. Others gather,
of course they do. The medical is contagious.
They know the heat I'm exuding, heat

that can't be stopped from rising. Tonight,
I want them to forget I'm a cardiac arrhythmia,
forget I'm a venous system, forget I'm necrotic tissue.
Tonight, I am sequins. I'm a lost clutch bag.

I'm a pay-as-you go mobile. These items
don't need a doctor. All I need is a full fat coke
and maybe a vodka. I need forgetting,
a loss of the conscious medical. I need her

to be a clueless civilian; questioning
if smelling salts work, if she should raise my legs;
if she should call an ambulance. She shouldn't search
for my carotid, for the stitching of my heart.

Tonight, she must remember I am sequins.
Yes, a pulse, and she makes it quicken.

Death Inc.

Do not be afraid. I'm sorry to say the worst has happened.
I don't know the circumstances of each of you, but my condolences.
There are fire exits in this presentation hall, but sadly they're ghosts also.
This isn't a space which is escapable, your life is just pretence now.
We here at Death Inc. cannot authorise refunds.

I'm here to inform you about Next, a new product for clients
in your condition. Please form a queue and start your Next policy
with an advisor after this presentation. Next is our new branding
for the afterlife. Next is the premier experience of death,
and you should feel lucky to be chosen.

Occasional one-off trips to Earth will be considered by application.
For a small fee you can appear in dreams, or dart into the corner
of a loved one's vision. But given trade secrets you're privy to now,
face to face visits cannot be facilitated. We're a small business, see.
A start up really. We want to keep off the radar for now.

Please understand. Fill in this survey
about the experience of life before you came here.
We know the difference between truths, so consider *everything*
before you answer. Naturally, these are monitoring forms
and will not affect your use of our product.

Breathing is an optional extra
for those looking to relive the glory days on Earth.
Unfortunately, you no longer shag or eat, but you don't need to shit
which is a bonus. What? Didn't expect me to swear?
Haven't you realised yet, where you really are?

Hide and Seek

My mother learns I'm in trouble when a nurse says *Resus*
like it rhymes with Dr Seuss. *Re-seuss*. He turns

the monitor away from me. My body writing
a tell-all-book, the hospital needs

to protect me from. I can feel my heart
blinking on that screen, flickering as my cursor.

The machine keeps alerting the staff towards
my apparent death. I'm too shallow

to be captured. The doctor spends fifteen minutes
trying to get a cannular into one of the branches

inside my arm. How many times does a blood pressure cuff
need to confirm my consciousness?

How many times do I need to tell my mother
which of my documents to burn?

post pandemic britain

our country pops   so many balloons   at 6pm
        millions of balloons overfilled   with relief
when the dead   have my face   and not yours

abandoned inhalers   are forgotten
        because the only thing   they underlie
    are bandages   in the first aid box
rare disturbances to breathing don't count   surely
            rare disturbances   to the forgotten
    cannot be used as a reason   to give a ventilator   to someone else

★★★★

there was an excel file   which ran out of columns
        rainbows curling despite lamination

a football match   murdered   a friend   I'd have met   five years from now
        because five years   is not considered a loss   something   stolen
such a fine silver locket   with too gentle a clasp

★★★★

food packages   contain two apples   half a block of cheese

        seven slices of bread   two tins of beans
        three potatoes   & a yoghurt
this is what a week is worth   if your legs don't work

I find a lunch note:

you are on your own   we recognise vulnerability
        and advise you see   no one
if you need urgent monetary assistance   the hotline for Personal Independence Payment
        is available   with the average hold time   of two hours
    listen to royalty free songs   you must talk   in the first ten seconds   of a call
        otherwise the operator   will hang up   if you're alone
    if you have no one   if you listen for the laughter of the children next door

turn up the radio   *do not worry about the electric meter*
     sometimes   *you find something beautiful*
in darkness

★★★★

My should-be friend is dead   so who am I   to complain
   I haven't climbed a hill   that all accessible paths
     have been overtaken   by holiday makers   buying ice cream
from the man   touching money   not washing hands
between customers

I haven't climbed a hill   haven't felt   bitter air   reaching
the top   of my lungs   I've wheeled around my bedroom
     for eighteen months   the only landmarks: chest of drawers
hospital bed   pink drip stand   medicinal cabinet   with a timer
        who am I

to say   masks are paper   and I am here   blue veins
   clearly visible   my smart price skin   so thin   my ink is visible
        who am I

to ask   you remember   my body
             wheeling in circles

Hospitalisation as the Drowning of Ophelia

Lying here, setting in resin.
Too tired to realise
my gown is open,
and I've a central line
of glittering IVs.

Fingers contracting,
blood stolen
and cleaned
like tarnished silver.
I border consciousness

as netting borders
being nothing.
They've removed
a whole fingernail,
a tiny sign next to it

out for renovation.
The flowers were gifts,
violets scattered now
to hide bruising.
Mouth open, air hungry,

evolution's last plea
towards living.
Lead powder
over blue lips,
eyes of mild alarm.

If this is death
then I am stunning.

Your Chest Aches Before You Stop Breathing

My stomach lining peeps
out from the surgical opening
like a flower. Fat petals of it,
blooming from the gap.
It completes its lifecycle of necrosis,
bleeds, blackens, drops off.
Acid mixed with pus, sediment
mixed with plant matter.
Held in the vase of my feeding tube,
thirsty, draining, beautiful.

****

Instead of a box of chocolates,
bring me a selection of saline flushes.
As you push each into a fresh vein
I'll tell you its undertones, manufacturer,
preservative content. Press each of my ribs,
locate the stress fracture – I am a piano
with only one note.

****

The prescription name for meth
is Ritalin. The GP hands it over
saying there is little else. My heart
a quivering animal, curled behind my lung.

****

This body doesn't know present tense,
always crafting its own eulogy, coating organs
in black. My mother thinks
she'll soon be in a pulpit,
that her umbrella will match her grief,
waiting in the boot of the car.

I Wear a Set of Lungs as a Necklace

I've never held an orange which has fully dried out, with its cloves loose
and falling apart. I only know fresh oranges, cloves displacing juice,
a candle wrapped in tinfoil, dolly mixtures on cocktail sticks, the church

at once-a-year attendance. The belltower is a place I'll never visit again.
Pulling joy with ropes after a wedding. When I lost myself they started
by using plywood, made a door wedge supersized into a ramp.

We parked in the vicar's space. I became a higher level of Christian –
martyr, blame-ridden, sinful. This happened because I didn't pray
during communion, didn't make a stained-glass window of my life.

Once my carer's belt got hooked onto my wheelchair,
and in a silent chapel she panic-farted. It happened because I can't drink
blood, or let Christ's flesh dissolve on my tongue. It happened as a trial.

It happened as a wake-up call, it happened because I had sex too young.
My body chimes as it wakes up. It's broken. Parents
have blank data spirals: if there is fault, it is creation.

Mermaids on the Brain

I'm sorry to have to tell you this over the phone,
but I've got your scans in front of me,
and I'm concerned that the mermaids

we've discovered aren't receiving the care
they need. Their scales are falling off.
This can be very painful, all wounds

should be bathed in salt water.
Is there anyone at home who can help
you scrape the limpets off their skin?

Your girls are gravely ill, so they can't
look after themselves. How often
do you have an aura preceding your migraines?

Gosh, that many? I'll refer you to a specialist
in playing conch shells. It's important
you don't pollute your brain

with any petrol-like substances.
This extends to pen ink, glue
from stamps, and all decorative glitters.

I'm concerned that I can't see any boats
in either of your hemispheres.
There isn't even the wreckage of one.

Commence a course of nails, once nightly,
an hour before bed. Your subconscious
will use them for the build.

I notice you've swapped life rings
for Seals. Whilst I understand
this is a temporary measure, their teeth

are icebergs – bacteria lays dormant
beneath the gums. Don't let anyone
get bitten, especially one of your girls.

I note the fisherman gave you a final warning
about the size of your nets. The hagfish
can't breed at the rate you're killing them.

Temporary Tattoos Come Off in the Shower

Pringles contain more salt than sodium tablets –
the cardiologist suggests I suck on them as I can't swallow.

The GP refuses to prescribe vasoconstrictors; so I gather
the edges of my bank account like a drawstring purse,
but there's barely anything enclosed.

My body doesn't enjoy systems. It's a rotting bushel of apples
becoming cider. The cardiologist has lost hope.

My stomach and arms are bruised from blood thinners.
I had surgery to become a snake – gained the ability to shit
into a bag connected to my abdomen. He takes
my blood pressure: we sit in silence.

The doctor raises his eyebrows. As an emperor,
this signs my death warrant.

Under One's Hat

My mother thinks my tongue is retractable tape.
That I reveal too much, that I'm not good
at keeping secrets. One of my friends said
the only reason he can keep things quiet,

is his body has the handy feature of forgetting.
Never registering which truths belong to who,
blank pages recorded in place of events. Part of it
is my inheritance. My nan is a lethal gossip.

I'm a witness to so many lives unspooling,
that I've stopped waiting for the Police to arrive
and collect statements. Truth is slippery.
There's a reason why water polishes riverbeds

and stones. I close my mouth around the things I know,
lock them inside of me as treasure.
I understand now, why NHS noticeboards
are laminated. It's because of blood.

Turns out, doctors can't keep secrets either.
They hide them, chirping, tiny birds nesting
in their desks; fed by a tiny paintbrush.

What Happened?

For those of us who live inside the air hangar, stripped down
for parts and sold; there's another dozen who sell their bodies whole.

I pawned my liver to a bear so he could feed his children.
My lungs were gifted to an Aurelian, who pinned them

next to other moths. I sold my radius to a medical student
needing experience in fractures. I auctioned my left elbow

to an aristocrat who put it next to his taxidermied caterpillar.
My shoulder is betrothed to a creepy dressmaker,

and this morning my bicep fell out, a fish now clubbed.
I stuff newspaper into the gaps left.

Padding my skin, a cabinet of slowly disappearing valuables.

Window Eating

After Grace Nichols

every now and then
i get this craving
for something sweet or salty
so go to the bakery at M&S
as a voyeur of scent
to listen for donuts
gaining their skin
in the fryer
to hold the warmth
of cookies in my nostrils
unable to partake

Womb in Monochrome

All I ever wanted was a family.
I was even prepared to marry
the semen. Did you know

it's the ejaculate which determines
the sex of a child? Today, the waiting room
is full of empty bedding, wombs

without occupants. They schedule
the childless on a Tuesday,
but forget to change the posters.

I'm reading an amber alert
for a rattle which is a choking hazard.
I lost my eggs to CT scans.

They split and cooked inside my ovaries –
all that arrives each month is yolk.
Local radio is mumbling *The Bay* –

Turn Up the Feel Good.
The nurse takes my blood pressure
Temperature is an accurate contraceptive.

Have you ever tracked your cycles?
Her question hangs in the clinic,
like a heavy, blood-soaked towel.

Wouldn't Be The Strangest Thing

I remember Googling if I could get Hepatitis C from dried blood.
The hotel towel I'd used to take my makeup off was covered.
I didn't have my glasses on, and by glasses I mean a wariness
I should always carry when not at home.

Hep C from a towel wouldn't be the strangest thing to happen to us.
And by us I mean the personal and physical as separate selves.
One is always covering for the other.
I go down to reception, they ask how I know it's blood.

I say *I know blood* and by knowing blood I mean I've stared at enough
hospital ceilings to wonder how blood had spurted two metres up.
And by wonder I mean I know it must have been an artery.
And by an artery I mean it's unlikely the patient is alive any more.

The hotel offers me a refund. I take it and head back to my room,
peel back the duvet and find a thong.

Hospital Corners

The dying are judged
by how cheery they are,
their lack of moaning –
for not becoming a ghost
before strictly allowed.

Their faces are pottery
spun, pliable, damp,
readying themselves
for fire. Nervousness
lost, unclipped,

identification forged.
Close your eyes.
Hand over your body.
In the end, everything's
cliché, except holding hands.

Bright Dead Things

After Ada Limón

Instead of a mushroom cloud
the walls peel, and every month
the paint changes from pink to red
and back. There's a ghost
inside this mansion.

It's the size of a peanut
and never gets the chance
to be human. The strings attached
to tampons fray before I can excavate them.
They implant into my womb lining,

become IEDs. Dreams explode
in my uterus. Dreams shouldn't
leave stretchmarks. Doctors take
amniotic fluid, spin it inside test tubes
until it thickens into French meringue.

I always lose my babies
to science. The nearest
they come to my arms
is toilet paper.

Planetarium

If you open a camera's exposure,
stars are revealed to circle the sky,
stirring the night. Their light
is sugar in a mug of tea –
sugar dissolving and irretrievable.

The doctors start with kind science.
Sand used to be alive. We build castles
with organic matter, the grit
of living between our toes.
My genes powder under scrutiny,

I scrape them into a bucket,
but their structures never hold.
Turrets have cracks, flagpoles
collapse, drawbridges never come down.
All doctors ever play with is my ash.

Bipolar Disorder Secondary to
Mitochondrial Encephalopathy

They cannot even gift me a personality untainted
by medicine. The illusion that I can deploy & retract emotion
as easily as claws. *I diagnose thee a mouth breather* I say *no escape*
here, it's going in your records. Assess bodies for symptoms
like fine, grey hairs – everybody has one.

★★★

My mother keeps asking if I'm depressed.
What about your sweat? she'll ask, *or how about*
your tears? Is something wrong with their water or salt content?
I'm holding a syringe above my thigh.
Antidepressants, anticonvulsants, antibiotics,
anti-sickness, a single glass of orange juice.

This morning I chalked *fine* onto my skin like a clown.
I am fine I say as I spring from my box. *I am fine*
now please push me back down into the darkness. I am forced
to savour mornings. My heart sinks this body if I don't appease her.
It takes one heart and two carers to change the world,
to change a person. Just two carers and a single wardrobe door.

★★★

I found my voice translucent, seeded between bible pages
like doubt. I overheard her, and watched on

from the landing not knowing how to stop her.
She trembled once – moments before I swallowed her,

held her captive in my throat. She screams at night,
tricks me, her prison guard, into sleeping, then roars.

She listens to the doctor and breaks out, unable to cope.
I set her alight, nestled between fragments in the log burner.

★★★

My father keeps insisting I can't get a tattoo.
That tattoos are mistakes he can't fix on my behalf.
For God's sake, don't get a green one he says *they can't laser
green ones.* He got his only tattoo at ten years old.

His friends wrote *love* and *hate* on their knuckles,
while he gave himself a small mole on his third index finger.
Regret can be as simple as a mole he said. But I won't be getting
a mole, so he can't be cited as an expert.

What if, Dad? What if we all get in a crash
and are so badly hurt they can only tell our wrists apart
because of the book I'll be holding forever. What if
I meet someone in a bar and they don't believe I actually wrote a book?

When I say this could be essential, I mean when
my disease progresses and I don't remember anything at all,
some care assistant, or even you, Dad, could point to my wrist
and say *you wrote that.* A wrist is more convenient

than a bookshelf. It'd be easy, Dad. To remind me
that I managed it. That one day when my spine crumbles
I'll have another waiting in Waterstones.
That I am not an SD card, and I cannot be rewritten.

★★★

I have never held a heart, or even seen one beating. I have never
performed an autopsy, but have whispered my fear of a neighbour to a
nurse before she drugged her. I haven't eaten birthday cake in six years,
but know grapefruit interacts with most drugs. I've never edited the past
on purpose, but have placed myself within still images in order to stay
around. I have never witnessed a sheep give birth, but have seen a mother
with her womb inside out. I have never driven a family car but have
driven a tractor. I have never been in an ambulance, but have lived in a
high dependency centre. I have never swallowed an apple whole, but I
have swallowed a grape. I have never been to space, but I've been so dizzy
I've felt the earth's rotation. Let me carve an animal, let me stand beside
a butcher and watch blood clot in puddles. Let me learn to deconstruct
without worrying about the knife, its being too sharp.

★★★

The newspapers are calling it an empathy crisis.
That an intangible organ between the stomach and chest wall
in every human has hardened. We've been to too many funerals.

The loveless are sewing machines. Empty of thread,
but still punching holes in cotton. Baths at 2pm
are frivolous. Avocado suites are back in fashion.

Orange juice ferments next to the space heater,
cartons are bursting like faces. If I fall and it isn't logged
in a risk assessment, did it even happen?

***

I have smokers' fingers from vitamin B
It makes urine glow in the darkness of my bladder.
The pillows are shielded by a single plastic sheet like sweaty foxgloves.
Morphine is being weaned, larger and larger strips are being cut
out of my shoulder. A three-year-old has drawn lipstick
all over her heart. Surgeons print another x-ray negative
instead of talking about its malformation. Ginger biscuits
are dispensed as medicine. Bread arrives as toast at bedsides.
Mothers have transformed into courtiers, their queens
have quick tempers. An Orchestra sits in the bay
wearing surgical masks. A harpist plucks
the space between her mouth and my own.

***

The televisions turn on automatically at 6am.
Instead of alarms there's a breakfast trolley.
The sicker you are, the nicer the ward.

High Dependency has Crabtree and Evelyn toiletries.
Intensive Care has a stained glass window.
Hospice has a separate room per patient.

So close to the borders of consciousness,
the staff are haunted. There's more artificial wiring
per person than veins or arterial systems.

My mother isn't allowed to visit –
but Colgate has gifted me an electric toothbrush
with a battery life of 72 hours.

***

I have taken to pruning myself before outings, so I don't kill
any unsuspecting children. My toes have hardened into puppets.
I direct people to talk to them instead of myself.

My bruises are inkblots therapists make me stare at. They say
there are no wrong answers. I am asked to rate the level of nothing I feel
on a feedback form. Except nothing is a barometer.

My stomach has shrunk to the size of six cashew nuts.
Condensation gathers around my body (a syringe)
and doctors shake me to hide this evidence.

***

All of my friends are pregnant, each of their bodies
a moon at a different stage of its cycle.

I cook all of them Kraft dinner, adding extra cheese
to increase their intake of calcium. One by one

these women evaporate from my life – illness attached
inside of me, a never birthed placenta.

***

The surgery phoned to say the nurse who gave me my flu vaccine

has gone missing; and I'm told to recite everything I remember.
At 1.17pm I typed up a poem.
At 1.32pm I googled if was or were are the correct grammar.
At 1.34pm I refreshed Twitter.
At 1.37pm I watched adopted brothers reunite after fourteen years apart.

My search results admissible in court, I realise how difficult
the human decomposition process will be to explain to a poetless jury.

I remember his uniform because his navy-blue scrubs were sewn
with white cotton and I told my mother about how tatty he looked.

He left between Ruth Langsford doing burlesque with a broom,
and ITV reporting on Megan Markle's miscarriage.

I want to check local news, but don't. This would break
with my usual character. At 6pm
dad checks the ditch at the side of our house.
At 10.30pm I go to bed; and tomorrow I'll wake,
arm still dead from the needle glancing off the bone.

Thanks

Thank you to Amy Wack at Seren, for helping this book see the light of day. Your edits have been incredible, and your support unwavering. Thank you also to Sarah in Marketing – for applying for funding pots and pitching events galore. None of your work goes unnoticed.

Thank you, reader. The support I have received across platforms is overwhelming. Be it on YouTube, Twitter, Facebook, Email, letter or in person; I keep a folder of kind words you have said about my work for the days my mind tells me I'm rubbish. They sustain me and help me to continue onward. If you take one thing from this book let it be this: even the dying are alive. If you're a reader with a life limiting diagnosis: I see you. Grieving your body is continuous, sometimes the pain is intolerable, it is never an act of cowardice to talk about your life. You can't control the reactions of others, only what you do with it. Both the physical and mental aspects of our lives are intolerable some days, and that is okay. Ask for help, someone is there to listen. You are not a burden.

Thank you to everyone who has gotten me to this point, both medically and poetically. I treat my body and mind as two separate entities most of the time, my body is an annoying failing bag of meat allowing me to continue life, whilst my mind is what I consider my actual self. Neither my mind nor my annoying meat would be alive without the NHS. I particularly want to thank Keith Jamieson, the NHS psychotherapist who saved me from myself. I must also mention Dr Sayer, the best example of a Palliative Care doctor. He has seen me through some particularly close shaves when my body malfunctions, thank you. There are so many doctors and departments I could list here to thank, so I name only a few here – the Mark Holland Metabolic Unit, my GP Dr Knox, Senior Palliative Care Nurse Margaret, Dr Craig of Radiology (who gets extra kudos for coming in to fix my very, very broken tube on his day off), Dr Fitchett of Cardiology, and finally, I need to thank St Mary's Hospice in Ulverston (especially lead nurse Helen), the charities Together for Short Lives (particularly Lizzie and Annie) and Hospice UK.

To my dear friend Lydia Allison. Thank you for the laughter and love. To Steve Dearden, for carving out safe and practical spaces to write for young people across the North, I couldn't respect you more than I already do. To Kim Moore, for allowing me access to the poetic world and showing me it can contain anything (including me). To Caroline Bird for your skill and empathy whilst pushing me in mentoring sessions, and writing past barriers of my own making. Thank you to both Poety Club (not a typo!) and The Dreamers for amazing peer support. Thank you to Wordsworth

Grasmere for continuing to fund the group which creates young poets across Cumbria. Thank you to The Northern Writers Awards (particularly Will Mackie, and the 2020 judge Vahni Capildeo), for giving me the confidence to say aloud "I am a poet writing my first collection". To Arts Council England, for giving me the funding to fine tune these poems and begin tentative steps toward new and evolving work. To The Society of Authors, for your emergency grant during the darkest depths of shielding from the Coronavirus.

Lastly, to my family. For your persistent and quiet hard work, I see and appreciate you more than I can articulate.

Poems Previously Published in:

'Comorbidity Isn't Death' – Bath Magg; 'Hide and Seek' – Poetry Society Website; 'I Wear a Set of Lungs as a Necklace' – Poetry Society Website; 'Mermaids on the Brain' – Poetry Wales; 'Post Pandemic Britain' – An ACE Funded Commission for Something Nowhere.

Earlier versions of 'Little Deaths' and 'We Created a Garden' appeared in my Verve Poetry Press Pamphlet, 'Where I'd Watch Plastic Trees Not Grow'.

An earlier version of 'Parents' was published in my Debut Pamphlet 'Dear Body' by Wayleave Press.